Did You Know?

Elizabeth S. Wolf

Rattle | *Studio City, California* | 2019

Layout and design by Timothy Green

Cover image by Allef Vinicius (CC0)
(⊙ seteales)

ISBN: 978-1-931307-40-6

First edition

Rattle Foundation
12411 Ventura Blvd
Studio City, CA 91604
www.rattle.com

CONTENTS

ACKNOWLEDGMENTS

"Tangled Web" appeared in the anthology *Merrimac Mic IV: Watershed*, March 2018.

The quote in "March 2004" is from *Millions of Cats*, written and illustrated by Wanda Gág. The first edition was published in 1928, by Coward McCann, Inc., New York, USA.

DID YOU KNOW?

Tangled Web

Before HIPAA
        before women could carry credit cards in their own names
        back when talking about birth control with unmarried young women
            could land you in the Charles Street Jail—
my mother's legs were tingling. Some days they felt
hot, swollen, and stiff; some days they didn't feel
much at all. My mother spent summer afternoons
sitting on her screened-in porch with bags of frozen vegetables
draped over her legs, needlepoint in hand, or a deck of cards
for a wicked game of bridge.

One fall my mother went blind in one eye.
But then her vision returned.

My father was a lawyer. We had
the best of Boston health care.
When my mother's primary care physician
and her consulting neurologist
and her ophthalmologist
concluded the most likely diagnosis
was multiple sclerosis,
they let my father know
over lunch, with drinks,
in town at the club.

My father was a first-generation
American, a bombardier in
World War II, a graduate of Harvard
back when there were quotas for Jews.
My father was the dictionary definition of
responsibility and competence.

My father was lost.

[...]

He sought counsel of his best friend, RM,
a fellow lawyer.

He sought counsel of his best friend, Dr. K,
now their physician.

He went before his formidable father-in-law
who had founded the law firm my father now managed.

Late in the fall of 1968
after bullets felled Martin and Bobby
after the Tet Offensive and the
Broadway opening of *Hair*
my father, filled with the best of
intentions, made an awful decision:
to keep my mother's diagnosis
a secret. From her.

Believing the stress of naming the disease
would make it worse, my father chose
to be her guardian, the gatekeeper
of incoming information. He would tell her
when the time was right. He was certain
he would know
when the time was right.

This was something he could do. He could protect
my mother. From her own body. He accepted that burden
as a husband's duty.

So my father signed up
her primary care physician
her consulting neurologist
her ophthalmologist
her father and her mother
many friends and cousins

and swore them to secrecy.

My father managed this whole conspiracy
flawlessly. Until the summer of 1975, when he unexpectedly
dropped dead. He was 50. His widow was 45.
His children were 22, 19, and 16.

My father left an insurance policy and an estate plan.
My father left no instructions for how to handle the secret.
And so
        it continued to be kept.

May 4, 1970

Because something is happening here
But you don't know what it is
Do you, Mister Jones?
　　　　　　　—Bob Dylan, "Ballad of a Thin Man"

When the National Guard killed four students at Kent State,
injuring nine more, my father was wounded. The dead looked
like his children. The National Guard looked like his children.
His government was shooting unarmed citizens. It was not
what his family came to America for. It was not what my father
fought for, trained for, decades before, flying missions over
Germany, upholding the oath of a bombardier before
he was old enough to vote. It was not right. He was not right.

For years, arguing with my brothers, my father had declared:
"When your country calls, you go." And, "My country,
right or wrong." What if it was wrong?

My parents had a big house in the suburbs, good schools,
a green lawn, a fenced yard. My brother's friends gathered
on the porch and talked about the war, about Nixon,
about the draft, about the bombs, about the lies.
Were the soldiers in My Lai only following orders?
Where had we heard that before?

My father locked the door between the porch
and the dining room; he opened the window between
the porch and the kitchen and passed out the black
rotary dial phone. He closed the window but for a thin
crack for the cord. The boys on the porch
became the local Kent State Strike Committee.

We skipped school. I learned to run a Gestetner mimeo machine,
making copies of leaflets to staple on telephone poles around town.
We organized sit-ins and marches; we shared food and clothes.

Sometimes I walked out the porch door and into the main house.
I did loads of laundry in the basement. I made sandwiches
and cookies. I walked out the kitchen door
and back into the porch. I was 11.

My father used to say there was nothing a girl could do
worth paying for. Girl talk was vapid. Back talk was verboten.

I was a ready recruit for the war at home.

The Center Did Not Hold

My oldest brother went to college
in the fall of 1970. For Thanksgiving that year,
my father flew my middle brother to visit on campus.
My father made vacation plans with my mother.
He told me, you can do whatever you want
for the holiday, as long as it isn't with us.
      I was 12.

I went to stay with a friend. I did that
more and more. I was the kid who came for dinner
and stayed three days.

The next Thanksgiving, my friend's parents
started bickering after the guests were gone.
What is wrong with this child? asked her mother.
It is Thanksgiving, and no one in her family
will speak to her.

I didn't stay there any more holidays.

I walked into the local multiservice center and
said I needed a place to live.
And so began
      the revolving gyre
            that lasted the rest of my childhood.

My father was fine to see me go. But
he refused to surrender custody.

In Massachusetts in the 1970s
anyone who housed a minor child
for three months could sue
for physical custody.

And so
        at least every ninety days
        (and sometimes more often)
            I moved.

Sometimes I was in foster care.
Sometimes I ran away.
Sometimes I stayed with friends.
Sometimes I ran away.
Sometimes I worked for room and board.
Sometimes I ran away.
Sometimes I went back to the land
with a cousin doing subsistence farming
but I couldn't go to school without
        a custodial adult.
And so the cycle repeated.

I was sent to boarding school.
I ran away.
I was expelled from boarding school.
And so the cycle repeated.

My father died. And still,
the cycle repeated. There was an even
higher law in play: a body in motion
tends to remain in motion.

August 8, 1974

My parents got a color television
after men walked on the moon.
Richard Nixon always appeared
a bilious shade of yellow-green.
"Don't adjust the set," my mother would say.
"That's just him." My father, Mr. Republican,
would object. My mother kept working
on her needlepoint.

The August that Nixon resigned, I was
at a friend's in Deering, New Hampshire.
Their summer retreat had no phone and no
television. We walked down the dirt road,
to the home Lotte Jacobi shared with
Beatrice Trum Hunter. Lotte was a famous
photographer: she took portraits of
Einstein, Chagall, Eleanor Roosevelt. Bea was
a natural foods maven: she provided
pesticide research to Rachael Carson for
Silent Spring. I did not know this then.
Lotte and Bea were neighbors; Lotte took pictures
of my friends searching for turtles or playing with
Breyer plastic horses. Watching that
historic speech with those incredible women,
I was thinking about

                arguing with my father,
if he would yell, if we would ever talk again. I was
a fierce rebel, completely unaware of the blinders
still solidly soldered to my eyes. I didn't know
women could be heroes.

Fall & Winter 1974

For my junior year, I was sent away to
prep school. Two hours west, with lots of
rules and a lovely chapel. School and
boarding combined. Problem solved.

In October I got sick.
I went to the infirmary but they said
I was seeking attention, and sent me away.

Two hours later I was back.
My temperature was over 103.
They let me stay.

My fever spiked, and my joints swelled
and ached. Finally the school doctor
called my father. "We are taking her to the
hospital tomorrow," the doctor said.
"They will most likely admit her."

"Boston is the medical mecca of the world,"
my father said. "If my daughter needs to be
in a hospital, she needs to be in Boston."

My father had a very important client meeting.
So they arranged for my mother to fetch me the
following day. The doctor called back later.
"Put a mattress in the back of the car," he suggested.
"Your daughter can't sit up for that long a ride."

My mother drove out with a friend. Someone helped me
to the mattress. We drove east. My mother pulled the car
into the driveway and locked it. I was in the back,
in and out of sleep.

[…]

My mother called my father. "I can't handle this," she said.
"It's too much for me. You have to come home now."

So my father left his very important client and drove
to the suburbs. My mother stayed inside the house.
I stayed locked in the car, in and out of sleep.

By the time we reached the ER
I was running 105 and delirious.

I spent three weeks inpatient with rheumatic fever. I could have
been discharged earlier but no one would take me home. I went
back to school with polyarthritis lingering in my wrists and ankles.
I spent Thanksgiving in the dorm, catching up on schoolwork.

In January the school had an intersession. I had signed up for
Spanish guitar and cross-country skiing. I could do neither.
The school refused to let me switch classes. The time period
for changing classes was closed.

"But I was in the hospital," I said.
"We have rules," said the dean.

Neither teacher wanted me present but benched.
"It disrupts the class," they said.
"We have rules," said the dean.

So the teachers told me not to show up
and not to get caught. Every morning I left the dorm
before 8 a.m. I did not return until after 4.

It was a cold and snowy winter
filled with structure and lacking any mercy.

July 23, 1975

My mother and father were at a golf course
on a sunny Wednesday afternoon in July. First tee.
My mother turned to watch my father's drive.
It never came. He lay on the ground at her feet.

After the ambulance, the ER, and gathering
my brothers, my mother called my school.
I was working as a mother's helper and taking
summer classes. That night we were on a field trip
to see *King Lear*, in Connecticut. Rather than
intercepting the bus and making me wait
at a state police station, they decided
to send my brothers to pick me up after the show.

I don't remember the play at all. I was restless
all night. Something, somewhere, was very
very wrong. The drama teacher scolded me
all the way back. When I saw two guys waiting
on the walkway, I leapt out of the van. I thought
it was time to party. When my brothers told me
what had happened, I didn't believe.

We drove south on Route 91 by the Connecticut River,
then the Mass Pike east towards Boston. My
mother was sleeping on her screened porch while
family friends waited for us. Just after 2 a.m. my mother
woke up and went to the back door. "My children
are here," she said, as we pulled into the driveway.

August 1975

After summer school ended,
I went to my mother's. I thought maybe
I could go home.

Two days later my mother stood in the doorway
of what was once my room. "My friend J is coming
to visit," she said. "I thought I'd put her in here."

"OK," I said. My mother stumbled as she turned
and wall-walked down the hall.

I left the next day. I stayed with friends
until the dorms re-opened in the fall.

Summer 1981

My grandfather used to gather his family
and close friends for milestone birthdays.
He would fly his daughters and their
families to a resort location and
ensconce them all in a fine hotel.

Except for me.

In 1981 he flew in my brother from California
and my cousin from Texas. I was in Arizona.
Too far, he declared.

I was hurt and angry.
I asked my mother and brothers
to stand up for me. "It's his party,"
said my mother. "He can invite
whoever he wants."

"Why do you want to go?" asked my
middle brother. "We don't."

"So skip it," I suggested.

"Can't," he answered. "It is a
command performance."

Before She Knew

My mother shopped for groceries
at the oddest hours, when she was least likely
to see anyone she knew. My mother had a
wobbly gait and needed to clutch the cart.
It takes a lot of steps to get through a supermarket.
My mother was afraid her neighbors would gossip
that she was always drunk.

When my mother did drink,
she used a paper cup. The nice glasses
from the bar set kept slipping from her hands.

Sometimes my mother sat halfway up the stairs
and halfway down, like the Christopher Robin poem.
I found her there reading more than once. She was afraid
one day her legs would fail and she would be stranded
forever upstairs or down.

Sometimes after she sipped scotch from her paper cup
my mother crawled. She was afraid if she fell down
she might not be able to get back up.

My mother got tired and napped often.
It stressed her out. My mother recited
nursery rhymes to soothe her worried mind.

My mother feared she was going insane.
She didn't tell anyone.
Her children were embarrassed and didn't say a word.

August 1983

My oldest brother, married and with a
baby, was moving to L.A. My other brother
was already there. I lived south of Worcester.

A cousin took my brother to lunch.
"When you leave," said the cousin,
"your mother will have no children left
in the east."

I don't know if my brother mentioned
that I was still in Massachusetts.

"Before you go," said the cousin,
"you should know: your mother
is sick. She has M.S."

My brother was stunned. "She never said!"
he protested.

"She doesn't know," said the cousin.
"Someone has to tell her."

The Wall Comes Tumbling Down

My brother called Dr. K
and said: "It's over. You
have to tell my mother
all about multiple sclerosis
and that she has it.
I can't tell her.
I don't even know
what the hell it is.
You're a doctor.
You can answer questions."

"What about her parents?"
asked Dr. K.

"They can't diagnose," said my brother.
"Take care of your patient first.
Then the rest of the players
can answer for their sins."

That Night My Mother Called Me

"Did you know?" she asked.
"Know what?" I responded.
"Did you know the secret?" she asked.
"What secret?" I responded.

Only my brothers, my mother and I
         and one true friend
had been unaware of her diagnosis.

Now there was an "us":
the ones who did not know.

And with that I was restored.

The Next Night My Mother Called

"I can't talk to my parents,"
she said. "I am so mad.
My mother came over with a hot lunch
and I didn't open the door."

"Good for you," I said. "You talk
to who you want,
when you want.
It's your house.
It's your life."

"Life sucks," said my mother.
"Also true," I replied.

The Following Night My Mother Called

It was very late. She was whispering.
"Your father's friend RM and his new wife
are here," she said.

"What the heck?" I responded.
"It's midnight."

"They called and wanted to come over
and I said no!" said my mother. "They called
again. I didn't answer the phone."

"Ma," I said. "You talk to
who you want,
when you want.
It's your life. It's under
your control."

"But they came anyway," she whispered.
"They are knocking at the back door.
I'm hiding under the window upstairs
in the study with the phone."

"Ma," I said. "You don't have to hide."
"What do I do?" she whispered back.
"Is the alarm on?" I asked.
"Of course," she said. "I was in bed."
"Ma," I said. "Open the window."
"But the alarm——" she started.
"Exactly," I said.

My mother put down the receiver.

[...]

Within a minute I heard sirens
followed by car doors slamming.

My mother hung up to call off the police.

My Mother Called Again

"I need a ride," she said.
"No one will take me."

"I will," I said.
"Where do you want to go?"

"I want to go to Sharon," said my mother,
"and stomp on your father's grave."

"Go ahead," I said. "It won't
hurt him. You do whatever
you need to do."

"No one will take me there," she said.

"I will," I said again.

"You can't," said my mother.
"It's not something I can ask
my children to do."

"Sure you can," I said. "And if it helps
I won't watch."

"Thank you," she said. "But no."

October 1983

While my mother's life imploded
I was flat on my back. That fall my doctor,
physical therapist, and chiropractor all agreed
it was time for surgery. There were no robotics
or microsurgeries then. A neurosurgeon literally
held your nerves out of the way while an
orthopedic surgeon reshaped vertebrae.
It was a big deal.

I lived alone on a lake. This was no longer feasible.

A friend was willing to house me for the months of recovery,
at her apartment in Atlanta. I first had to stabilize from surgery
in Boston.

My mother offered to take me in. She moved a stretcher
into her living room. Until I was well enough to fly.

The first time I was alone in her home, the phone rang.
It was her cousin, the one famous for welcoming family.
Except for me.

Cousin said, "We don't think you should be at your mother's.
It's too much for her right now."

I said, "Oh! Your invitation must have gotten lost in the move.
I've barely unpacked. I can be ready in an hour, if you want
to pick me up and bring me back to your house."

The cousin spluttered and stammered.

I said, "Oh! You thought I had lots of options! I don't, really.
I am leaving as soon as I can. Until then, my mother
invited me to stay here. And I think right now is a
good time to let her decide what she can and cannot do."

There Used to Be Rules

My mother told me once, when I was in my 30s,
she couldn't imagine how hard it must be to
have choices. In her day good girls were virgins at their
weddings, and that was that. And then the '60s
happened, and free love, and then in the '70s,
abortion was legal. Without the pregnancy card,
the whole game was changed.

My mother had rules for everything. Always
side with your husband. Be courteous
to the help. Tip the mailman and the paperboy
at Christmas. Towels are folded in thirds.
She knew what to wear and when; what to
serve for lunch or brunch or dinner; what to
wash in hot or cold. Her sheets were ironed.

I was visiting my mother in the mid-'80s when
she stopped outside the bedroom door.

"What do you think?" she asked.
"About what?" I wondered.
"Did you see?" she asked.
I looked around the room.
"Look at the bed," she said.
So I did.
"Look harder," she said.
So I did.
"I used the top sheet from one set
with a different fitted sheet," she declared.
"I thought you'd get a kick out of that."

I stared at the bed.

I stared at my mother.

[...]

She was positively delighted with her act of rebellion.

My mind reeled. How sheltered was she? What did she see
when she looked at me? Does she know how I lived as an
outcast, a foster child? Nights with no place to sleep, I crashed in
shelters, wards, hallways, under bushes, in
borrowed sleeping bags. I fucked friends
for a place to sleep.

But here I was, over 21, and she was wearing an ankle brace,
swaying on crutches to stay upright. The whole game
was changed.

I accepted her gift.

"Wow!" I answered. "I thought I woke up
extra spunky. Now I know why!"

She turned and crutched down the hall, giggling.

I stood staring at the space where my mother had been.

Circa 1986

For years after my father died
he was mailed the most amazing offers.
Life insurance, no physical required!
Credits cards, with low low interest!

Sometimes we considered cashing them in.
But at some point the scheme involved stealing.
So mostly the junk mail was recycled.

When Discover was launched, they mailed my father
a real deal. No annual fee. Sky-high credit limit.
My mother crossed out his name, wrote in hers,
and sent it back.

Two weeks later she was notified
her application was rejected.

Incensed, my mother called the 800 number on the letter.
"You offered credit to a dead man!" she exclaimed. "And then
refused a woman who has paid all of her bills for years!
That's sexist."

The operator promised the management would reconsider.

Two weeks later she was notified
her application was accepted.

My mother cut the card in half and mailed it back,
with a note. You made your most generous offer
to a man who has been dead for a decade. I wouldn't want
to patronize a company like yours. And she signed it,
Most Sincerely.

May 1986

After the secret came out,
I was included. But still
second rate. My grandfather
flew us all out to San Diego
and got hotel rooms for everyone.

Except for me.

I wasn't hurt or angry.
I was amused. I camped with my
brother and my cousins and raided
the hospitality fridge.

"Seems the great and powerful
'man behind the curtain' is afraid
of me!" I marveled. "Just what superpower
do I secretly possess?"

After She Knew

My mother did a lot of research.
She chose all new doctors. My mother
joined support groups and signed us
all up for newsletters.

My mother moved to accessible housing,
with mobility aids, within two years of the
conspiracy collapsing. My mother named her
crutches: Fuck and Shit.

My mother enrolled in a clinical trial.
They gave her chemo to knock out her
immune system. She lost her hair and
never walked again. She spent two months
in a rehab hospital. They spread lined sheets
over her bed and chair, in case of accidents.

My mother pinned the sheet to her
shoulders like a cape, threw off her
wig, and raced down the hallways
full tilt boogie in her cherry red Rascal.

My mother was a rocking superhero.

July 1993

When my grandfather died,
lawyers wept. The family
held a roast, presided over by his
younger daughter, at a hotel
by the funeral home,
probably on his dime.

It made me a little uneasy.
"It's just not right," I said.
My aunt said, "Let's have a
contest. Who did he say
the worst thing to? Who did he
treat the most badly?"
My grandfather hadn't spoken to me
in years. I went home.

The next morning over breakfast,
my aunt told me I was declared
the winner. "But I wasn't there,"
I said. "Exactly!" said my aunt. "You
were excommunicated, dear.
Shunned. Cast out."

I took a sip of coffee and waited.

"Did you know, when your father died—"
"When I was 16," I chimed in—
"Exactly. Well. Your grandfather, my father,
declared you were such a bad daughter,
it killed your father. And that's why
he so suddenly died."

I was stunned.
"Really?" I asked.

"Truly," she answered. "Neither man
thought you did enough
to take care of your mother. "

"I was a child," I said. "And, I didn't know
that she needed to be taken care of."

My aunt reached for her purse.
"Did anyone ever tell you?" she asked.

"No. Not until this very moment," I replied.

My aunt poured a nip bottle of Grand Marnier
into her cereal bowl. "There," she said.
"You won."

March 1997

I got married at 38.
My mother was so happy.
Vindicated. A sure sign the
damage was remediated.

We eloped. I got married
barefoot on the beach,
with witnesses. No family attended.

My mother threw us a cocktail party
a month later. She insisted that we
register; her family and friends
wanted to buy us gifts.

"Ma," I said. "I don't live in a rabbit hutch.
We each have our own place.
We have sheets. We eat off of plates."

"All the world loves a lover!" she sang.

But your family hates me, I thought.
They would step over me down on the ground
to make it to the movies on time.

My mother spent the weeks between the
wedding and the party in the hospital. She
checked out early to meet with the caterer.

We registered at every store she suggested
and sent thank you notes promptly,
without being asked.

March 2004

The last time my daughter and I visited
my mother, we didn't know it would be
the last time. My daughter was four.
We decided to stay over, since I've never
liked driving at night. We made up nests of
foam pads and sleeping bags in the drive-in
guest closet.

After the home health aide tucked my mother
into her tidy bed, we joined her. I got out a book
I had brought: *Millions of Cats*. It's one of the only books
I remember having read to me as a child. She told me
her mother had read it to her.

My daughter snuggled between us.
We chanted the chorus:

> *Hundreds of cats,*
> *Thousands of cats,*
> *Millions and Billions and Trillions of cats!*

My mother had one hand to her
mouth. Her eyes were full. The other hand
reached out tentatively to stroke the book.
It was really there.

April 2004

By the end, before she died,
my mother forgave them all.

Except for my father.
She hated him.

Her parents, her cousins, their friends,
Dr. K and his wife, all of them visited
her condo, borrowed best-selling books,
and watched cable movies
on her TV in the den. They all admired
photos of my daughter, the only grandchild
in the east.

Hundreds of people attended her funeral.
Dozens delivered eulogies
lauding her grace and her courage.

Except for my father.
He remained dead.

Also April 2004

My mother's children
were not so quick to forgive.
We gathered at her condo
before the memorial service,
going over the lists of people
who had been notified, or
called, or sent food, wondering
who would show up.

"X won't show," said one brother.
"Already called for time and directions," I said.

"Surely not Y," said the other brother.
"They were here for dinner three weeks ago," I said.

We went through her old address book, asking
only one question, over and over:
What did they know
and when did they know it?

April 2005

After my mother died
I was diagnosed with stage 0
breast cancer. The doctors
recommended tamoxifen.

I was leery. I asked the
hospital librarian for a
literature search.

As I was leaving Baystate
Medical Center, I saw my mother
in her scooter, with her post-
chemo gray hair, shaking her head
no, no, no.

Then I remembered she was dead
and she was gone.

I refused tamoxifen.
I told them I decided based on
reviewing the research.

Thanks, ma.

April 2007

Turns out marrying the anti-father
was also not the right answer.

I had married a man with perspective, who remarked
as an ambulance passed: somebody's life
just got changed.

I had married a man addicted to drugs, who stole from me
and said money didn't matter, that I knew nothing
about being a family.

When our condo burned down, he made it clear
he didn't light the match.

While I was getting divorced
my mother's friend and her sister
were my supporting elders.

"My mother wouldn't approve," I said.
"She considered divorce a demerit."

"Nonsense," said her friend.
"Your mother wants that man gone."

"Nonsense," said my aunt.
"Your mother is standing with you."

Two nights later as I was getting ready
for bed, I noticed some papers on his dresser.
They were the receipts for checks he had
forged in my name. I had spent an entire
weekend searching for those check stubs.
I called anyone I thought could help me locate
or recreate them. I wanted tangible proof.

To this day I have no earthly idea
where those chits came from.

I sent them to my lawyer, attached to an affidavit.

Thanks, ma.

Recycling the Travel Section

My family always read the newspaper.
When we sat for dinner—6:30 every
weeknight—you better know your news.
Sunday papers were a special treat.

For years after the secret was spilled
my mother separated the Travel section
from the Boston *Sunday Globe* and sent it
unread to recycling. If she had known, she said,
she would have traveled. With her children.
My mother loved London and always
wanted to return. You can't get that back.

And all that time estranged
from her children, fighting her own
decline. Some things can't be fixed.
Splintery shards remain, like the glasses
that slipped from her numb hands onto
cold hard floor.

Ma, if you're still listening: I have taken
my daughter to the ends of the earth.
California. London. Aruba. India. We saw
sunrise at the Taj Mahal. We have hiked
in the Amazon rainforest, and on top
of the Great Wall of China.

Ma, if you still care: I carry a piece of your
jewelry with us, wherever we go.

And in the End ...

... the love you take
is equal to the love you make.
—*Lennon–McCartney,* The End, *1969*

Many years later, I saw on a website
that my grandfather's firm was sponsoring
my local women's shelter. I emailed my
father's friend, RM. He must be spinning,
I joked.

Your grandfather believed in pro bono, wrote
the lawyer, and in giving back.

Did not know that, I replied.

Every year they give out a judicial award
in his name, wrote the lawyer.

Did not know that, I replied.

And so in 2010 I went as a guest of the firm
to the Boston Bar Association award reception.
Afterwards we went to the Parker House for dinner.
My daughter wanted me to bring her a
Boston cream pie.

"So," said the lawyer. "You have a pre-teen.
I wish your mother could see this. What's
it like, being on the other side? You put your
parents through hell."

I stared at him. "That was a long time ago," I said.

"Did you ever talk about it?" he asked. "Did you ever
apologize to your mother?"

I reached for some water. "No," I said. "Once the secret
came out, we never looked back. We had
other priorities."

"Oh that," said his wife. "That didn't go on for very long."

I stared at her. "About 15 years," I said. "Eight of them
after my father died."

The lawyer stared at an empty chair. "I remember
the day your father came into my office," he said.
"He was a broken man. Your mother was his life.
He didn't know what to do."

"Anyway," said his wife, "there was no treatment then,
so it didn't matter. It wouldn't have made any difference."

I realized they knew the secret
but not the story.
I was their guest.
I was my mother's daughter.
I spoke slowly and gently.

"You can tell yourselves whatever you need to,"
I said. "But know this: you were part of a pact
that violated the do-no-harm clause. And all of us
were changed."

We sat in silence for a few minutes, and then
talked about headlines in the news. I ordered dessert
to go.

About the Rattle Chapbook Series

The Rattle Chapbook Series publishes and distributes a chapbook to all of *Rattle*'s print subscribers along with each quarterly issue of the magazine. Most selections are made through the annual Rattle Chapbook Prize competition (deadline: January 15th). For more information, and to order other chapbooks from the series, visit our website.

www.Rattle.com/*chapbooks*